MW00795126

The Awakening

Book of Poems
Bare Emotions of Love, Growth & Self-Worth

By

Sharika K. Forde

Watersprings
MEDIA HOUSE

THE AWAKENING
Published by
Watersprings Media House, LLC
P.O Box 1284
Olive Branch, MS 38654
www.waterspringsmedia.com
Contact publisher for bulk orders and permission
requests.

Copyright © 2017 by Sharika K. Forde

All rights reserved. No part of this publication may be
reproduced, distributed, or transmitted in any form or by
any means, including photocopying, recording, or other
electronic or mechanical methods, without the prior
written permission of the publisher, except in the case of
brief quotations embodied in critical reviews and certain
other noncommercial uses permitted by copyright law.
Printed in the United States of America.

ISBN-10: 0-9988249-09
ISBN-13: 978-0-9988249-0-1

To My Four Sons

Four Little Angels

The first blessing came at the age of eighteen
In one flash, you appeared
And it seemed to be a dream
Now God has given me four angels to keep
I kneel down and thank Him every night before I sleep
Your brown eyes are so precious
Your innocence so unique
From infants to toddlers to young men
It's amazing to me
I've watched you grow
And pray that the world treats you fair
I hope the hard lessons are far and few
And are easy to repair
My four little angels
I thank you for the lessons I've learned from you
Just a touch or caring words can heal all wounds

TABLE OF CONTENTS

☥

ACKNOWLEDGMENTS

First, I would I like to thank God for blessing me with the gift of poetry. Life has taken me on many journeys and through all of them there were lessons to be learned. I didn't always pick up on the lesson right away, and at times I had to repeat a journey for the lesson to really be learned. Still, I stand thankful and proud of the woman I've grown into.

I would like to thank my Daddy. He raised me and my brothers as a single father. As a little girl, I felt I was different from other girls because they had moms or grandmothers. However, I watched my dad go to work every day and provide for our small family. From that, he taught me responsibility and strength. Now that I'm a parent myself, I respect him more than any other person on this earth for instilling those same qualities in me which I pray are carried down to my children. I also would like to thank all my family and friends who have supported me when I was single, married and then single again. Whether big or small, I will always appreciate the time we spent laughing and sometimes crying.   To my first grandchild, Jaciah, I pray that your world is filled with love and joy.

Finally, to my four sons, Janeil, Jaquan, Jamari and Jaheim. Each of you are different, each of you are special and each of you are loved. Please know that everything I do, say and feel reflects my love for you. Live your dreams, recognize your strengths and utilize the gift that God has blessed you with...we all have a gift.

Chapter 1

sensitivity

Stand in My Shoes

Sometimes I feel invisible
I wonder what people see
Do they see past the surface
Can they see inside of me
Can their face see the pain that's
Imprinted on my soul
It doesn't seem that way,
from what I am told
They say I'm always happy,
always in a good mood
But if they read past the surface
and stood in my shoes
They would see the fear that's inside of me
The confusion in my eyes
They would hear the lies that I've heard
And understand why
Why I sit quiet at times
And don't want to be spoken to
They would understand why
If they stood in my shoes

Mommy Dearest
(In Memory of my mother RIP)

For many years I have walked this earth
12-7-73 was the day of my birth
A baby girl added to a family of four
A mommy, daddy and two brothers would share my world
But something happened
Five years later the family fell apart
Mommy was on drugs
And daddy found another woman to share his heart
Too young to understand what was going on in my life
I just knew that things weren't right
All the arguing and fighting, things had changed drastically
Now I wondered what would happen to my family
One brother and I were left
On the steps of my father's mistress
We were taken into her house and lived with her kids
But that didn't work and my father had to raise two kids
In the confusion I learned
That my oldest brother wasn't his
But he showed up at our door one day
Running away from life with mother
And I was happy to finally see my oldest brother
Life had seemed to go back to normal
Only one piece was missing from the puzzle
Mommy was on her own
It had been years since I had seen her
Then one day I received a call
It was something I couldn't ignore
Mommy went to heaven, she died in her sleep
And the family was brought together to weep
I was nineteen and didn't know how to feel
It seemed like the funeral wasn't real
Mommy was gone
I didn't get the chance to say goodbye
I didn't get the chance to tell her how much
I wanted her in my life

My Heart Cries Loud at Night

My heart cries loud at night
But no one hears the sounds
No one sees the tears
Or the clouds that hover around
A hidden emotion
Which I choose not to share
Not wanting others to see
That I'm affected in this way

Stay strong, hold your head up
And put a smile on your face
When asked "How are you?"
Say "everything's ok"

My heart cries loud at night
The only time my strength is allowed to break
My only time of freedom
From the responsibilities of the day
When the sun shines
My shield goes up to get me through the struggle
My shield is my protection
And gets me over the hurdles
But it's becoming weak
And my heart is crying louder at night
It's a struggle to keep up the strength
To continue the fight
When darkness falls, the shield's lifted
And emotions pour from within
A cleansing of my soul
A release of the frustration

Child with No Name

(16 years old)

The seed that grew inside of me
Changed my life completely
I turned to you for support
And you destroyed all my hope
We laid together and made a baby
But then you deserted me
The sex, you couldn't resist
But claiming too young to handle this
Turning to my father for one last hope
But his eyes spoke his words
The decision wasn't mine to make
It ended in one day
Stolen away through abortion
And I hated you for not supporting me
Years later I still feel the pain
My first child had no name

Lost Soul
(2nd miscarriage)

From day one of the discovery
Of this life inside of me
I gleamed with joy over bringing home
An addition to our family
Thoughts of a girl ran through my head
Colors of purple and pink
Names like Janae, Serena and Chyna
Cluttered my mind
Hair bows and braids
And little girlie games
I thought it would happen this time
With one doctor's visit, everything changed
They said there was no heartbeat
And I was left alone
In a cold doctor's room to weep
People said "it will be ok, you can always try again"
What if again doesn't come around
What will happen then
A child was lost
I was frozen in time
To everyone else, it was just a phase
I should be proud of what I have and move on
Does that mean I shouldn't care
That a part of me is gone
Vanished as if my imagination
Created a bad dream
But a dream it was not
And I will never forget
The day I lost my baby

Wish I Was Dead

Sometimes I wish I were dead
Maybe then you'll be happy
At least I won't be here to blame for this catastrophe
Maybe then you can enjoy all the things that we gained
Without me here creating any pain
But the cut wasn't deep enough, it just broke the skin
Next time I'll cut deeper, maybe it'll work then
Then I'll be laid to rest from these years of neglect
Perhaps then you'll realize the pain that I felt
My feelings for you were true; I loved you with all my heart
Maybe dying is the only thing that can break us apart
Tell my children I love them
But my life wasn't meant to be
Make sure you tell them
They were not the cause of my misery
And to my husband I want to say, I'm sorry for the pain
I really thought love could conquer everything
And to my family, I'll miss you, but please don't cry
This was something I wanted-- I just wanted to die

Fragile Heart

They say I'm mean and selfish
And don't seem to give a fuck
But that's just my way
Of protecting my fragile heart

My bluntness is a defense
To keep you at bay
So I won't have to mend my fragile heart
From getting hurt someday

My trust is my word
I honor those who show mutual respect
And keep those untrustworthy away
So I won't have to face neglect

I've been there, done that and realize
Not all relationships are meant to last
Still, I protect my heart from future pain
Because it's as fragile as glass

Chapter 2

anger

The Pursuit of Happiness

How do you pursue an emotion
That you never had before
It's like waiting for a stranger
To walk through your door
Searching for the unknown
But knowing it's what you need
Searching for a feeling
That is beyond your reach
In pursuing happiness
Will I forget the hardships of the past
Once the chase is over
Will I pursue something else fast

What To Do

Insecure about myself
I'm not sure what to do
Feeling useless about myself
Not knowing what to do
Sorry about the way things are
Ignoring what to do
Hopeless about our future
Afraid of what to do

Broken Vows

This is my last plea
To change our destiny
And I hope you realize
How much your actions hurt me
I tried to understand and stay by your side
But in the end
My feelings just got pushed aside
We don't communicate or relate anymore
I already have my bags packed
With one foot out the door
The situation that I'm trapped in
Is suffocating and taking all my life
I'm not sure you did the right thing
By making me your wife
My heart was broken into pieces
And it can't reconnect
Did this marriage turn into
Something we regret?

Love Changes

My words your words nothing will ever change
I look in your face and it's not the same
Something has changed; it has torn us apart
Now that something is damaging our hearts
Without a clue you left
In search of someone else
Now I'm here all alone to care for myself
Your return was too late
We both changed from the past
And I realize that our love would never last

We tried over and over but just couldn't get it right
We tried over and over and still ended up in a fight

The signs were all there
But we ignored all the rules
We thought our love would be strong enough
Despite all the clues
Then one day it happened
You just walked out the door
It finally ended
Our love was no more

When I Cry

When I close my eyes
Thoughts of you enter my mind
When I open my eyes
No one is there and I'm left standing alone
When I speak of love
Memories of you resurface
When I speak of heartache
Your name is the first to leave my lips
When I lie in bed
I wonder when the pain of love lost will vanish
When I cry at night
Its tears from your abandonment

Reality Check

Crying out for you
My voice echoes around the room
The emptiness that's inside my heart
Is taking over my mind
Learning to live alone
And face challenges day by day
Without you by my side
To help me laugh, cry and feel
I wake up and open my eyes
To learn my nightmare is real
Another day of loneliness
Has been brought before my eyes
I put my hands together
And pray that I will survive

The Decision

The decision was mine to make
I thought letting you back
would fix the mistake
But the minute after you walked
back through the door
A sensation came over me
that I could not ignore
It felt like stress, tension and despair
The feeling somehow was familiar but rare

For the first time my heart
was speaking to me
Telling me that our relationship wasn't meant to be
I turned around and changed
The decision that was just made
And decided you needed to go on your way
The amazement in your eyes
strengthened me to stand true
And I could picture a happy life without you

Now instead of holding on to security
I ran for independency
in hopes to find sanity
The decision made me realize my true destiny
That happiness in life lies truly within me

Chapter 3

clarity

Final Goodbye

I heard you left, but you didn't say goodbye
I wonder if what I felt was a waste of time
The connection seemed to be real
But now I'm left with mix feelings
I heard you're working and finally living well
I'm glad you were able to get out of your living hell
It's been a few months
And my feelings for you
Just won't go away
I keep hoping you'll come back to visit
And I'll see you again some day
Not to restart our relationship
That opportunity has passed us by
I just want to be able to say
A final goodbye

Letter to TC

Dear TC,

I found myself sitting up late one night writing this letter to you Hopefully one day you'll be able to read this and know how I really feel When we met years ago, you treated me so good But fresh out of a bad relationship, I just wasn't ready for you My mind knew you were the one, but my heart wouldn't let you completely in And I have spent these years trying to find what we had then

I love how you treated me I love how you respected me I love your gentlemen ways and how you tried to protect me

We ran into each other one day and you asked "If I ever thought about you" The answer to your question years later is "I do" I watch movies and thoughts of you enter my mind As I pass by the park, I think of you every time And every year during the first week of December, I gear up to celebrate In the excitement, I never forget that you are also awaiting your special day

I know many years have passed and I'm not writing this to cause any drama or strife I just had to let you know that you will forever be a part of my life

Love & Blessings
skf

The Introduction

Tall, brown skin with dreads
He stood before me like a King
The introduction was soundless
Through his eyes he spoke
The glare of a lion
Staring down his prey
Searching for a response to his eyes
But not knowing what to say
As our paths crossed again
We felt emotions of excitement
A room filled with people
But only two were united
Both knowing what they wanted
But thought it was too soon to try
Both in need of affection
Eventually their bodies collide
Afterwards, laying quiet
Neither wanting to speak
The introduction that led to a simple end
Parting with a kiss on the cheek

Love to Love

I use to shy away from love
Afraid of the pain it would cause
Now I yearn for that feeling
But it seems it is lost

I want my heart to beat fast
I want my legs to shake
I want to think of you when I sleep
And when I first awake

It's that feeling you get
When you can't live without that one
That one you placed on the pedestal
And can never do any wrong

I want to reach my arms around you
And hold you so tight
I want you to lay by my side
Each and every night

My heart is open for you to enter
Just say the words
I feel a pain within my soul
But your love will cure it all

Let Me Love You

I just wanna love you
But you're afraid
to let me into your heart
It was something I noticed
From the very start
But I held on hoping
It would only take a little time
I held on knowing
That one day you would be mine

Just let me love you
I know you've been hurt before
Your past emotions are holding you back
From moving forward
Don't mistake the position
God has put us in
This thing between us
Is no coincidence
You made your way into my heart
The feeling is so raw
It's the sweetest thing on earth
Because it feels so pure

Just let me love you baby
That's all I wanna do
I wanna show you off to my girls
And say "yeah that's my boo"

From Old Love to New Love

My first love passed by me
My heart skipped a beat
As our eyes crossed paths
We sat to catch up on the present
And reminisced a little on the past
He made me think of my new love
Brown eyes, tattooed arms and waves
It's funny, after all these years
My taste in men still hasn't changed

Beautiful

Your face
Your hair
Your smile
All so beautiful

That laugh
That walk
That style
All so beautiful

From the top of your head
Down the crease of your back
To the bottom of your toes
You are so beautiful

I Wish

Holding your hand
Softly touching your face
Looking in your eyes
While words of passion
Flow from your lips

Holding you tighter, closer
Not wanting to let go

Feeling your gently hands rub my body
A light touch between the legs
Sends my heart beating faster
And I crave for more

Our bodies combine as one
Our passion fills the room

I wish to give you all of me
I wish this feeling last forever
I wish you were mine and I were yours
I wish...

Chapter 4

blood, people & land

African Pride
(For Black Men)

Come out from behind your disguise
Show me your spirit
That African pride
Warrior...Leader...Statue of Glory
Somewhere deep in your eyes
Tells the story
From childhood to manhood
The history runs deep
You close your eyes to dream
But you can not sleep
Troubled by the path
Your future might take
Wondering if you'll live to see another day
Dreaming of things that the white man stole
Trying desperately to find a way
To make them your own
You need to know
Your woman will be by your side
To hold you up and encourage
Your dreams and your desires
You are blessed with a vision
Only few can see
You are my heart, my soul...My African King

Lost One

Braided hair
Baggy pants
Tattooed from arm to arm
Slurred speech
Ghetto slang
Black hoodie keeping you warm
Through quite days
And hard nights
You stand tall and hold your own
With thoughts of your ghetto Queen
Keeping you strong

She's had your back
Through it all
Now she wants you to leave the game
Afraid that her ghetto King
Will be taken from her one day

Lost to the streets
A world she hopes you'll escape
Promise after promise, you tell her
The day will come when you'll walk away
Night after night she cries
Until you return the next day
Option two, leave the state, create a new path
That takes more money
Which means more streets
Just do the math
A circle of deception
That's how the game is mapped
Many young brothers lost
In the white man's trap

Poor Black Female

You see me with one child on my hip
And one holding my hand and think...poor black female
You see me at the register
paying for my groceries with food stamps
and think...poor black female
You see me with my kids at the playground
 with no daddy to be found
And think...poor black female
What you don't see is my hustle
 to provide for my family
As i carry one child
And hold the other tightly
The food stamps i use
To substitute for cash
is not abuse
After struggling and working hard all day
This is the only way
To off-set my low pay
The fatherless play you see
Is a family enjoying a moment of serenity

So please think before you judge
I answer only to the One above
He guides my life and my decisions
Living for him is my only mission

Next time you see me
instead of thinking poor black female
Think...
God has blessed her
With the strength to do it all

Strong Black Woman

Her spine bends slowly
From the weight she carries
Expecting neglect and mistreatment
Making sure her mind and body
Are strong enough to receive it
Being daughter, sister, wife mother and sometimes father
Makes her seem untouchable to others
Afraid to break down
Because she's known for holding her own
Afraid to show that this strong black woman
Still has some growing
The outside stays polished
Prepared for anything that comes
The inside seems irrelevant
And stays hidden from the world
A world that constantly tries to break her race
It started with the white man's rape
Raped from our country, ourselves and each other
We followed the pattern not knowing any better
Hoping to breed strong children with hopes and dreams
Working hard to keep her family
Away from crime and poverty
It's a weight that gets heavier as the years pass day by day
She gets down on her knees every night and pray
She looks for a strong black man
To help get this weight off her back
Then realizes his weight is sometimes heavier
Being a black man in America
Memories and the pain has been embedded in her
Even throughout captivity
She is the picture of strength, peace and sensitivity
It is the Strong Black Woman you see

Black Love

Writing my thoughts down everyday
Helps to release the pain from my memory
Every day the feeling is becoming weak
Writing is the only way to speak
The words flow from my fingers in ways I can't explain
It's similar to a mastermind in a video game
There's only a few who understand my point of view
And the rest I find just don't give a damn
Or are afraid to see the truth
It's a shame what it comes to
But there's not much I can do
Supportive of those who just can't see
That it takes much more than your word
To get out of misery
You have to fight for your rights and have to stand tall
And be prepared to get back up in case you fall
These times are confusing, especially for our youth
Trust me, with four sons, it's easy to see their view
We have to aim high to make a future for them
And show them the way to fight the prejudice
Use your brain not your fist
The power is already instilled in you
Because our ancestors and parents had to fight too
Sometimes it seems in vain, have we grown from the past
Sometimes it seems useless, the hate will always last
Love yourself, improve yourself and show others the way
Unite ourselves, teach ourselves and study our history
One day we'll reach the top and set our own rules
One day the power will shift
Then others will know what we've been through
Black power we'll scream from the top of our lungs
Black love of all kinds; lawyers, nurses and youngins'

One Love

The pattern seems to grow stronger day by day
We see ourselves in the mirror
And don't recognize the face
Jealousy and envy
Have been the death of many
And still we breathe off hate
Instead of feel pity

What happened to "fight for your rights"
and "black power"
The movement is a memory of the past
We exchanged raised fists with raised guns
And thrive off black on black violence

Ebony tone and yellow bone
Why aren't we united as one
Suited up or baggy jeans
The fight has only begun
African braids or straightened hair
Our style is not to blame
Single mother or loyal wife
It's the same at the end of the day

Read, write, think
And acknowledge your history
Martin, Malcolm and so many others
Died for what we have achieved

My Straight Hair

Love the pics of all my chics
Sporting their natural hair
But can I relate, my hair is straight
Does that mean I'm less aware
Compliment one chic with a natural do
Received a "thank you" and crooked stare
Followed by "try it, be the real you show no fear"
Yes! To kinky curls, No! To creamy crack
It's a battle only black girls feel
Created by us, imposed by us,
Are we truly "being real"
Judging the inside by outside appearance
Should hairstyles make a difference
Love as one, Unite as one
There's power in acceptance
Encourage our brothas, support our sistas
Our preference is our uniqueness

Straight hair
Standing strong
Head down
One fist up
Pride for my African Heritage

Not Our Sons!

Raising 4 sons I was told by a "friend"
Of the statistics of their success
They said at least one son will be on drugs
Or end up under arrest
I replied, not my sons!
With a bang to my chest.

Basketball, baseball, football and track meets
Anything to keep them off the streets
Building bonds with the community
Meeting other moms, doing the same thing
Changing the statistics
Raising kids with drive and ambition
Not Our Sons! We Scream.

39

Chapter 5

the awakening

The Star Within

There's a star within you
If only you would let it shine
It's funny how negative things control us
And take a hold of our minds
You think you don't deserve more
And are willing to settle for less
If only you could see what I see
You truly deserve the best
I noticed it from the first day
The shining star within
From that point on I knew
You would be a treasured friend
I hold you close to my heart
And promise to never let go
Through tears, hugs and laughs
My love continues to grow

Champion

Put down the balls
And step away from the field
It's not in the way
You throw or catch
So please let go of that shield
It's not about your looks
Or any sexual feelings
It's what's inside of you
That have formed this connection
You have a heart of gold
And through it, all your emotions show
At times, it's beyond your control

Vulnerability shows you care
Fear is something we all share
Strength has allowed you to carry-on
Confidence put you on the path for continued growth
Your imperfections show you're human
Acceptance of self shows you're healing

Your emotions have allowed me to look deeper within
The bond goes beyond friends
For this, in my eyes, you will forever be a champion

Letting Go

I realize I have to just let you go
But my heart keeps fighting my mind for control
When I think about you everything feels so real
But with your situation, my patience just can't deal
You say you want to spend time with me
And get to know me well
But every time I try to get close
You have an excuse to bail
The sweet sound of your voice, the soft touch of your lips
Keeps me from seeing the truth
But these weeks without you and no phone calls
Has allowed me to see the true you
Your priority is the streets and making cash
My priority is love & finding someone who makes me laugh

So alike but so different, I thought our worlds could unite
So alike but so different, it seems to be a constant fight

Now I know, I just must let go of this love I feel for you
I'm letting go of the dream and I need you to let go too

Family Tree

Received a call from my oldest son
Voice shaking with fear
Young black male, age 21
I braced myself for what I was soon to hear
The words came out slow
And I questioned what I heard
Asking him to repeat it again
Pregnant...Baby...Girlfriend
My mind begin to comprehend

Mother at 18, Grandmother at 39
A new family timeline has emerged
Wanting to yell at him, but resisting the urge
Saying relax and breathe instead
Babies are a blessing
God's plan is ahead
This is what was meant to be
A tiny branch added to our family tree

A Reason

I'm losing the thoughts, the emotions and the taste
The memories are becoming a lot easier to erase
I listened and tried to make it work out
But still I'm unhappy and realize I need to give up
I thought it was meant to be, the way we came together
Until I received an email, it spelled it out a little better
A reason, a season or a lifetime it said
It defined different relationships and cleared my head
There was a reason for you and me
I just have to figure out what
I'm sure it will come to me
When I'm not buried in thoughts

Now it's been settled, I must move on
And learn from what we had and apply it to my next goal
With no regrets, I thank you, for the time that we shared
I feel that I'm ready and fully prepared
Prepared for the next relationship
Now I really know what I want
I want what we had, plus so much more
The reason, it's there, it didn't take much time at all
I figured out the reason, now I can finally move on
For I hope the next one will not be a reason
But a lifetime instead
I'm ready to give my heart to someone
Who truly deserves it

SHARIKA K. FORDE

My Naked Body

As I look at my naked body
There are two scars that stand out from the rest
One is on my wrist and the other on my stomach
The creation of these scars
Came from different circumstances
One was to save my life
And the other was to end it
I will look at these scars for the rest of my life
And remember two days of pain
One from a child who wasn't strong enough
And the other from when I didn't want to live again

Now as I look at my naked body
I realize God had other plans
Instead of my life ending on those dreadful days
I was given another chance

The Awakening

Found myself falling
Into a deep sleep of depression
Questioning my strength
To combat the emotion
Blood flows through the brain
In wild patterns and directions
Searching for a way
Out of this congestion
Finally
A rebirth has taken place
And now I can see
There is an exit
Out of this insanity
Self love, respect and confidence
Will be the guide for me
The eyes to my soul are open
I am finally set free

THE BEGINNING

ABOUT THE AUTHOR

Leading her life by love and laughter, Sharika K. Forde has a passion for creative expression. She started jotting down notes of poetry many years ago. Her journey to self-worth began as a senior in high school when she became a teenage mother. What began as a form of personal healing, she now shares her poetry to awaken others to bare their gift. She is a mother, aspiring entrepreneur and a student of life. She discovered that the challenges we face are lessons that evolve into discovery of self. Beginning each day with prayer for good health, monetary wealth and true love, she strives to live a life of fulfillment through her passion for creative artistry and continual growth.

Email: theawakeningpoems@gmail.com
Website: www.theawakeningpoems.com
Facebook: The Awakening Poems
Instagram: @SharikaKForde
Twitter: @awakeningpoems

CPSIA information can be obtained
at www.ICGtesting.com
Printed in the USA
LVHW082144121220
674058LV00022B/297

9 780998 824901